Enjoy Playing Guitar

Tutor Book 1

First steps in playing classical guitar

Debbie Cracknell

MUSIC DEPARTMENT

OXFORD

UNIVERSITY PRESS

OXFORD
UNIVERSITY PRESS

Great Clarendon Street, Oxford OX2 6DP, England

Oxford University Press is a department of the University of Oxford.
It furthers the University's aim of excellence in research, scholarship,
and education by publishing worldwide

16

ISBN 978-0-19-337134-7

Music origination by Julia Bovee
Printed in Great Britain on acid-free paper by
Halstan & Co. Ltd, Amersham, Bucks

All pieces are original compositions or arrangements by the author unless otherwise
stated. The following copyright holders are gratefully acknowledged:

(Meet) the Flintstones
Words and Music by Joseph Barbera, William Hanna, and Hoyt Curtin
© 1960, 1962 (Copyrights Renewed) Barbera-Hanna Music. Administered in the UK &
Europe by EMI Music Publishing Ltd, London, W8 5SW. Reproduced by permission of
International Music Publications Ltd (a trading name of Faber Music Ltd). Administered
in the World excluding UK & Europe by Warner-Tamerlane Publishing Corp. Used by
Permission of Alfred Publishing Co., Inc. This Arrangement © 2011 Barbera-Hanna
Music. "The Flintstones" is a Trademark of and Copyrighted by Hanna-Barbera
Productions, Inc. All Rights Reserved including Public Performance.

Match of the Day
Music by Barry Stoller
© 1970 RAK Publishing Limited. Licensed courtesy of RAK Publishing Limited.

Preface

Welcome to this revised edition of Book 1 from the series *Enjoy Playing Guitar*. This popular tutor book for classical (or Spanish) guitar has been updated to meet the needs of today's beginner students. It is designed for use with a teacher, in group or solo lessons, but also encourages self-directed learning outside and during lessons. The material takes the student through notation and the basics of guitar playing in a carefully paced and logical progression. It aims to develop the all-round musician through improvisation, composition, and playing by ear, and introduces the art of accompanying using chords or ostinatos. It encourages good solo and ensemble playing using carefully selected tunes, namely well-known, popular tunes and original compositions tailored to specific technical demands. Finally, the CD (inside the back cover) is for easy reference and enjoyment, while learning at home, and for developing fluency. The features of Tutor Book 1 are as follows:

Tunes	• over 70 enjoyable and varied pieces, including traditional favourites, TV showtunes, and original compositions, all with helpful tips on performance
Exercises	• to consolidate technical and theoretical points, and as preparation for pieces
Flexible arrangements	• chords, ostinatos, and written-out accompaniments for the teacher or second pupil
	• rounds for 2–4 players
	• more complex guitar accompaniments on the CD, for home, school or concert performance
CD	• recorded demos of the tunes, for listening and play-along practice, including all the duets and trios
	• click-track intros of two bars (including any upbeats) for all demo tracks
	• recorded accompaniment parts, as backing tracks only
	• tuning notes on Track 1: each open string played three times, from string 1 to string 6
Quizzes	• helpful revision of music theory and knowledge of the guitar—educational and fun!—and questions for further aural training, using the CD
Illustrations	• detailed drawings for developing technique, showing correct posture, finger positions, and pitfalls to avoid
Note Banks	• prominent and helpful reminders of which notes have been learnt and when (these usually occur at the ends of sections)
Chord Diagrams	• a one-stop guide (at the back) to chords found in this book, for accompanying and improvising activities

Debbie Cracknell, 2011

The basics

Parts of the guitar

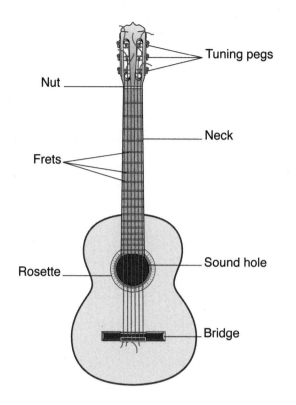

How you play—how you sit and use your hands—is important. A good technique avoids bad habits and ultimately improves your sound. The following illustrations show what, and what not, to aim for.

Sitting position

Always use a footstool (or other support) to raise the guitar to the correct angle.

Right-hand position

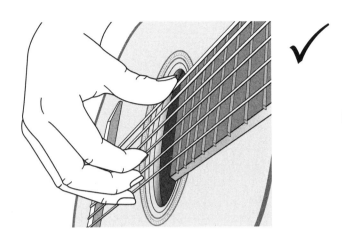

Keep your wrist arched slightly away from the guitar.

Your thumb crosses in front of the fingers.

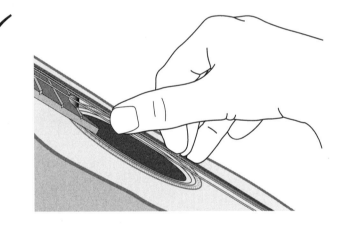

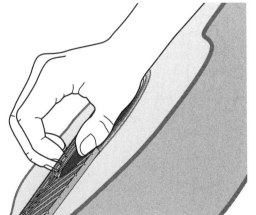

Don't have a lazy wrist.

Left-hand position

Keep your knuckles in line with the fretboard, curl up your fingers and play on their tips.

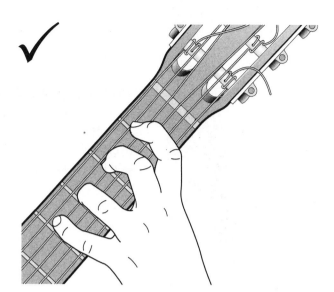

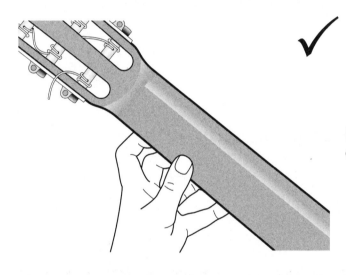

Keep your left-hand thumb well down the back of the neck.

Don't do it like this!

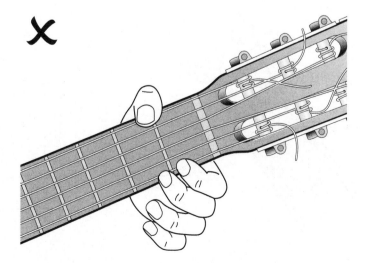

The rest stroke

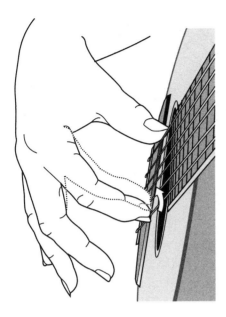

The finger strikes across the string and comes to rest on the next lowest string. Practise with *i* (index—*indice* in Spanish) and *m* (middle—*medio* in Spanish) fingers alternately on the first string (E), producing a walking action. Resting your thumb on string 6 will help keep your hand steady.

Try copying short rhythmic phrases on E (string 1) played by your teacher. Then try the same on B (string 2).

Now play: EEEE   EEEE   EE
                BBBB   BB

Make up your own short tunes using E and B and ask others to try and copy.

Strings and frets

Strings and frets can be shown in a diagram. The grid below shows the first four frets and the six strings of the guitar:

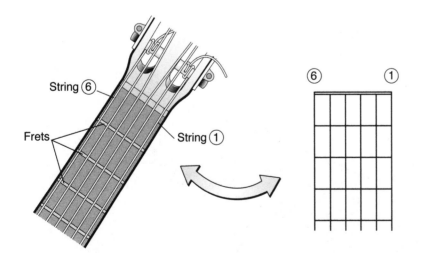

The first string

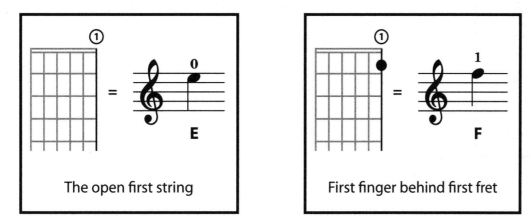

The open first string

First finger behind first fret

Music is written on a **stave** (five lines), and notes E and F occupy the top space or line of this stave. Guitar music always has a **treble clef** (𝄞) at the start.

Play the following pattern:

We're now ready to play our first pieces. Note that music is divided into **bars**, their length indicated by a **time signature** at the start of the stave. The top number in the time signature tells you how many beats to count in each bar, and the lower number, the type of beat. In this case, the lower number (4) identifies the beats as **crotchets** (or **quarter-notes**).

Two-Note Hop

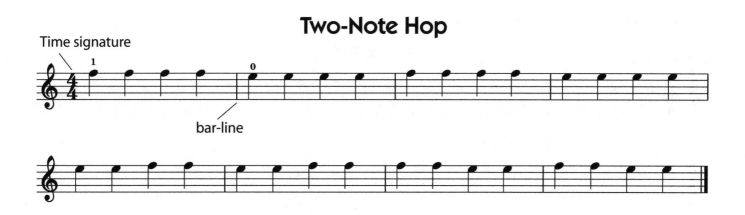

Time signature

bar-line

Two-Note Jump

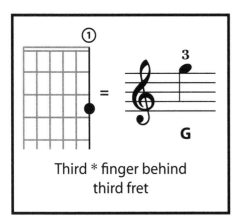

Third * finger behind
third fret

* An alternative fingering is to use fourth finger (little finger) for this G.

We have now learnt three first-string notes: E, F, and G. Play the following, but leave first finger down when playing G in bar 3:

One bar of E   one bar of F   one bar of G   one bar of E

Leave first finger down.

- Your teacher could invent short phrases using E, F, and G for you to copy.
- Now make up phrases for other pupils to copy. Music often uses repeated notes, so try this when improvising (making up) your phrase.

Tunes using E, F, and G

2: demo

March

Accompanied

(2-bar intro)

||: :|| are repeat marks and mean you should play each line twice.

4: demo

Jogging
Accompanied

(2-bar intro)

Once learnt, the above three tunes can be played one after the other to form 'A Little Promenade Suite', perhaps as a concert item. The backing track for this suite is 🔘 track 5, which has a two-bar intro before each tune.

Counting

♩ =	one beat, a **crotchet** (or **quarter-note**)	
♩ =	two beats, a **minim** (or **half-note**)	

1

2

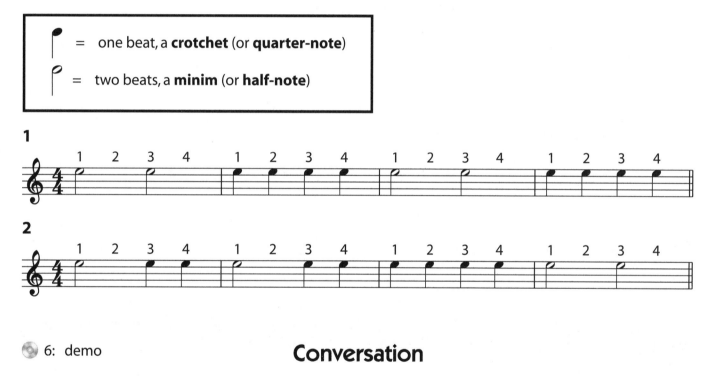

6: demo

Conversation

Write your own tune using the rhythm below. Begin and end on E and give your tune a title.

....

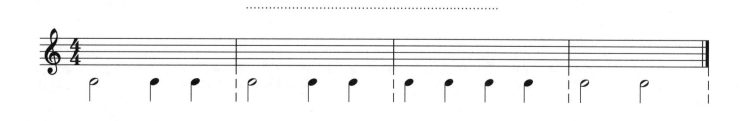

A new time signature

You already know that the top number in a time signature tells you how many beats to count in each bar. Let's turn our attention to 3/4, another time signature using crotchet beats.

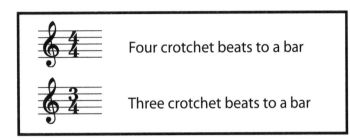

Four crotchet beats to a bar

Three crotchet beats to a bar

Clap or tap the following rhythm, emphasizing the first beat of each bar:

Now do the same with three beats to a bar:

Try the following exercises:

1

2

 7: demo

Waltz

The second string

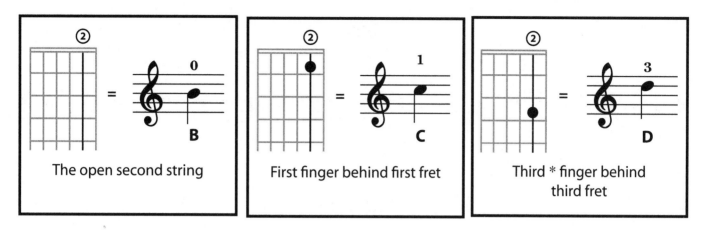

The open second string	First finger behind first fret	Third * finger behind third fret

* Some teachers may prefer fourth finger.

Bees and Cees

I. C. A. B.

Bees and Dees

Is your thumb well down the back of the neck?!

Tunes using B, C, and D

8: demo   **Solo**

9: demo   **Copycat**

Duet

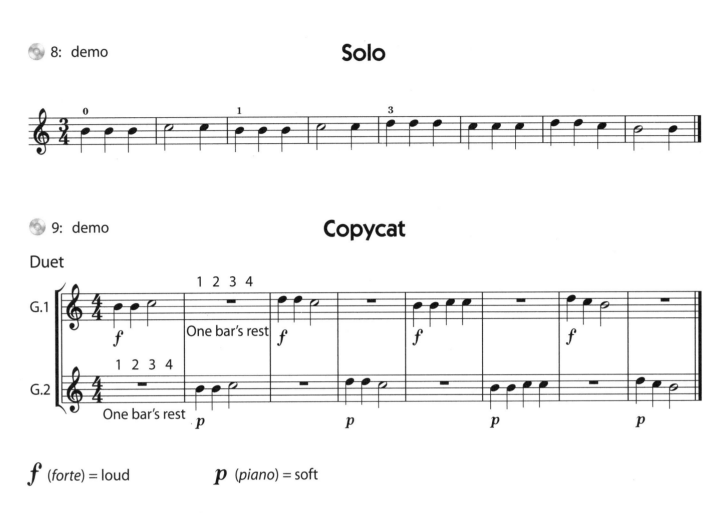

f (*forte*) = loud   *p* (*piano*) = soft

10: demo   **Echo**

From this point on, the Note Bank will remind us which notes have been learnt and where to find them on the guitar, quickly. It shows the string and fret information for the pieces you have played.

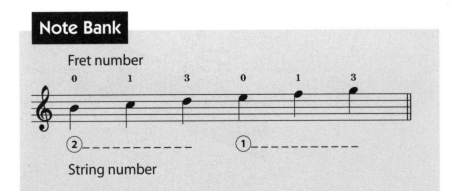

Counting rests

A **rest** is a symbol for a period of silence. You can produce a rest by damping the string with your 'next' right-hand finger to stop the note from sounding. In the piece 'Copycat' (p. 14), you saw the whole-bar rest. The next rests you need to learn are the crotchet and minim rests:

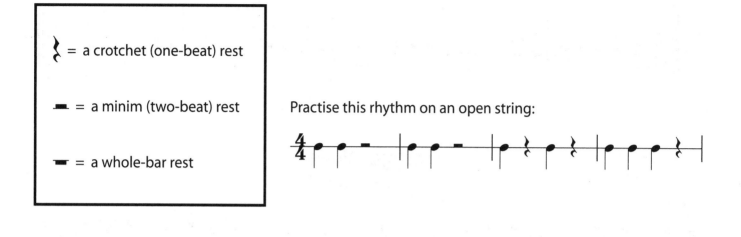

𝄽 = a crotchet (one-beat) rest

▬ = a minim (two-beat) rest

▬ = a whole-bar rest

Practise this rhythm on an open string:

Tunes using the first two strings

11: demo

Slow Train

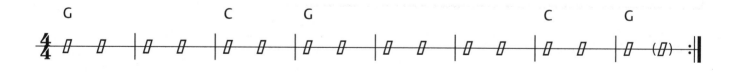

For accompaniment, try strumming three-note chords C and G, two per bar, as indicated below (see Chord Diagrams, p. 60):

12: demo

Go, tell Aunt Nancy

Trad.

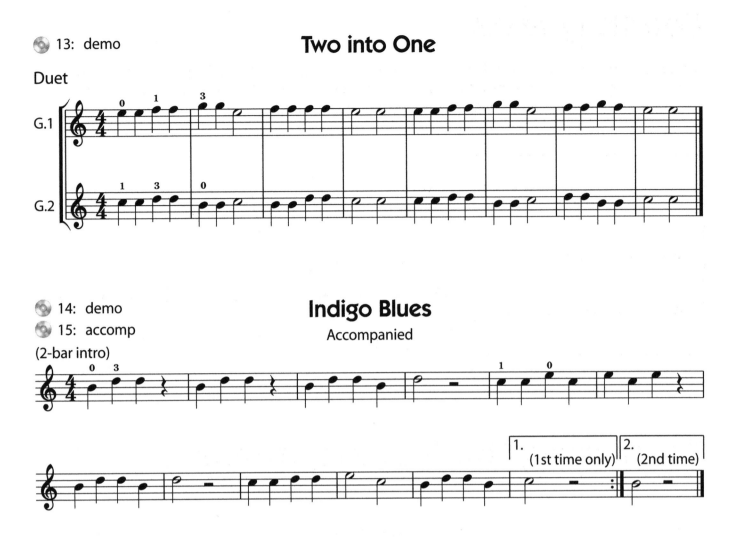

13: demo
Two into One
Duet

14: demo
15: accomp
Indigo Blues
Accompanied
(2-bar intro)

1. (1st time only) 2. (2nd time)

More on counting

= three beats, a **dotted minim** (or **dotted half-note**)

= four beats, a **semibreve** (or **whole note**)

16: demo
Little Bird
Trad.

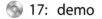 17: demo

Jingle Bells

James Pierpont

Old Time Minuet

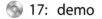 18: demo

Try adding strummed chords to 'Old Time Minuet', using the following rhythm (for new chord G7, see Chord Diagrams, p. 60):

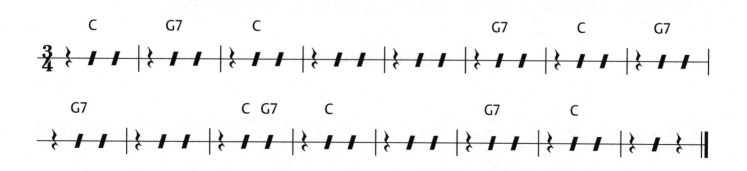

The third string

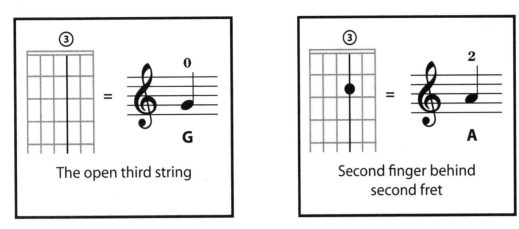

The open third string

Second finger behind second fret

Try copying short phrases using G and A played by your teacher. Try again, this time without looking at your teacher's fingers. Listening and copying in this way is called 'playing by ear'.

Exercises

1

2

Music uses the letters A to G in the alphabet. When reaching G it starts again from A. You now know all the notes from the middle G (open third string) to top G (third fret, third string).

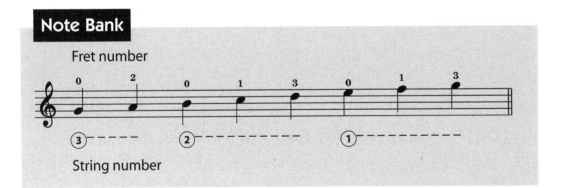

Note Bank

Fret number

String number

Tunes using the first three strings

19: demo

Yankee Doodle

Trad. (American)

20: demo

Au Clair de la Lune

Trad. (French)

You can add a **descant** (a second melody above the tune) to 'Au Clair de la Lune' using only E, F, and G on string 1, and by keeping to minims. Ask someone to play the tune while you work it out, or use the recording from the CD.

21: demo

Good King Wenceslas

Trad.

22: demo

Dance

Duet

The open bass strings

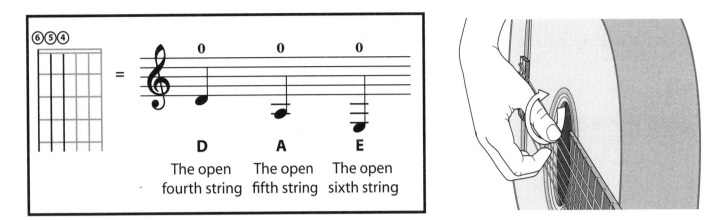

The right-hand thumb (called *p—pulgar* in Spanish) will usually play these notes. Strike it across the string in front of the fingers using a circular motion that moves from the wrist joint. Keep the thumb straight and do not rest it on the next string.

23: demo
24: accomp

(2-bar intro)

The Low Down

Accompanied

25: demo

The Russian Girl

Duet

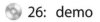 26: demo

Barcarolle

Duet

$\textbf{\textit{mp}}$ (*mezzo piano*) = moderately soft

$\textbf{\textit{mf}}$ (*mezzo forte*) = moderately loud

Note Bank

Fret number

String number

Open bass strings plus treble notes

Remember your right-hand position!

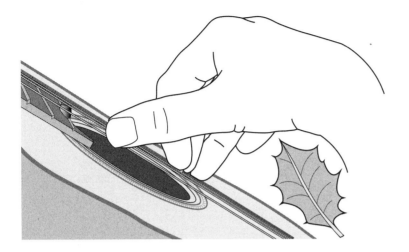

Is your right-hand wrist held
away from the guitar?

For pieces that use the thumb and the fingers, guitar music is usually written in two parts or **voices**. The stems go up for the finger notes and down for the thumb notes.

Before tackling the next pieces, try the following exercise:

27: demo

Thumb, Finger, Finger

28: demo

Serenade

29: demo

Inca Dawn

* Strum with the index finger (*i*) from string 3 to string 1. This gives a three-note E minor (Em) chord.

Summary of all the open strings

Write a sentence using the open string names as the first letter of each word. A silly sentence will be more memorable!

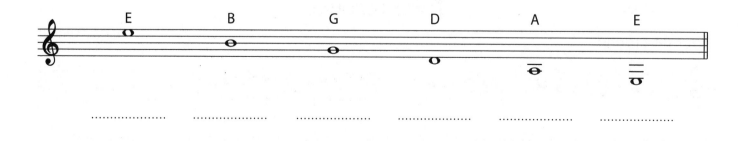

Introducing quavers

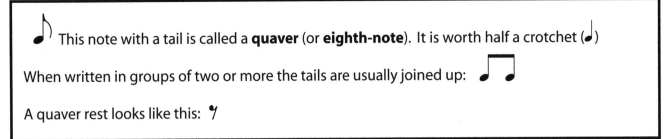

♪ This note with a tail is called a **quaver** (or **eighth-note**). It is worth half a crotchet (♩)

When written in groups of two or more the tails are usually joined up: ♫

A quaver rest looks like this: ♪

For counting in quavers it's useful to think 'and'. Try the following exercises:

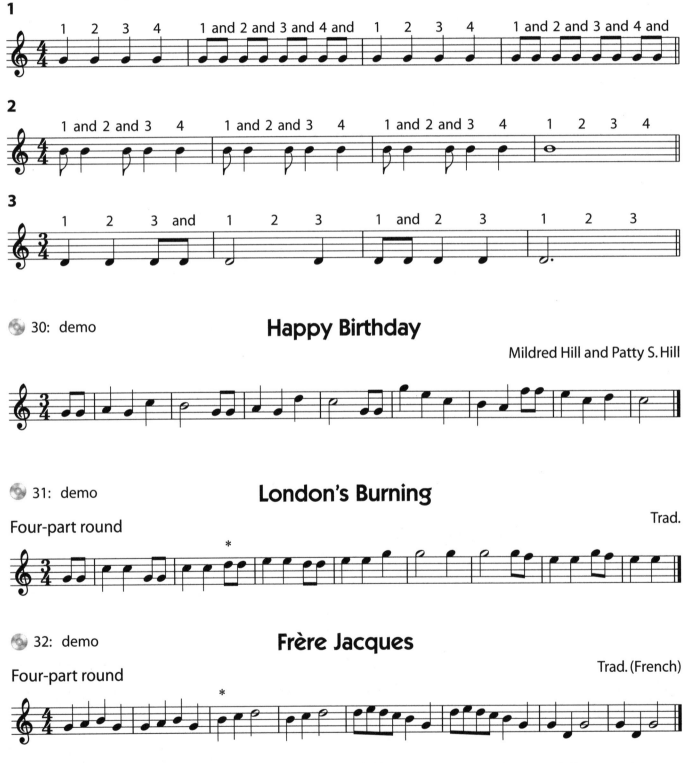

1

1   2   3   4   1 and 2 and 3 and 4 and   1   2   3   4   1 and 2 and 3 and 4 and

2

1 and 2 and 3   4   1 and 2 and 3   4   1 and 2 and 3   4   1   2   3   4

3

1   2   3 and   1   2   3   1 and 2   3   1   2   3

💿 30: demo

Happy Birthday

Mildred Hill and Patty S. Hill

💿 31: demo

London's Burning

Four-part round

Trad.

*

💿 32: demo

Frère Jacques

Four-part round

Trad. (French)

*

Play 'London's Burning' and 'Frère Jacques' as rounds, with further guitars coming in at *. You can also accompany 'Frère Jacques' (the melody or the round) with a G chord throughout.

33: demo

Oh Sinner Man!

Trad.

Accompany using the part below, or strummed chords of Am and G in ♩ or ♩ beats and following the symbols (see Chord Diagrams, p. 60). Alternatively, play all three parts together to form a trio.

Accompaniment

34: demo

A March for Two Guitars

Duet

For a bass-note rest, damp the string with your thumb.

35: demo
36: accomp
(4-bar intro)

Home on the Range

Accompanied

Daniel Kelley

The Tie

This line ties two notes together. Do not play the second note; leave the first note to ring on for the total of the two.

37: demo

Summer Waltz

QUIZ 1

1 Fill in the missing words:

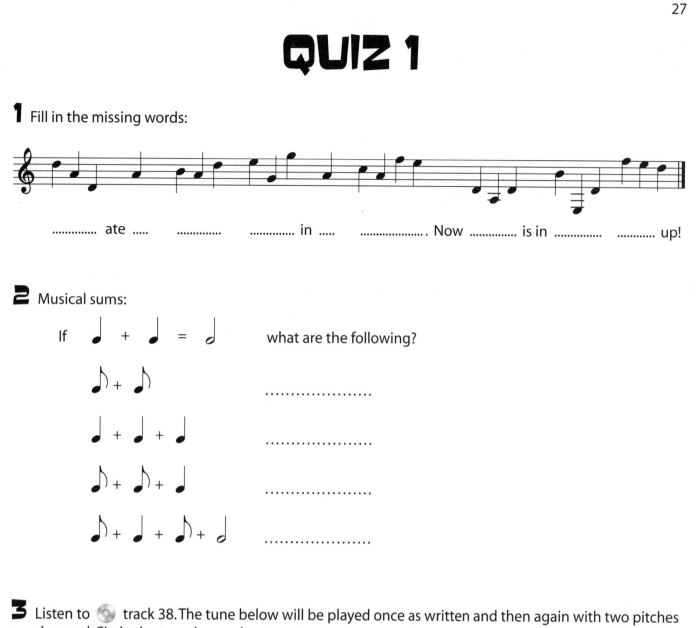

.... ate .... in .... Now .... is in .... up!

2 Musical sums:

If ♩ + ♩ = ♪ what are the following?

♪ + ♪ ....

♩ + ♩ + ♩ ....

♪ + ♪ + ♩ ....

♪ + ♩ + ♪ + ♩ ....

3 Listen to 💿 track 38. The tune below will be played once as written and then again with two pitches changed. Circle the two changed notes:

4 Tick the correct meaning:

♩ = ☐ a minim
   ☐ a golf club
   ☐ a crotchet

forte = ☐ a castle
   ☐ heavy
   ☐ loud

𝄽 = ☐ a minim (two-beat) rest
   ☐ a crotchet (one-beat) rest
   ☐ a seagull

② = ☐ finger number
   ☐ a coin
   ☐ string number

5 Listen to the two tunes on 💿 track 39. One of them has three beats to a bar (3/4) and the other has four beats to a bar (4/4). Which is which?

Tune 1 is in .... Tune 2 is in ....

The free stroke

After striking across the string, lift the finger up slightly to avoid the next string. Move the whole finger, not just the end joint, so that the finger doesn't 'hook' the string upwards. Use the free stroke when playing plucked chords and arpeggios.

The right-hand fingers

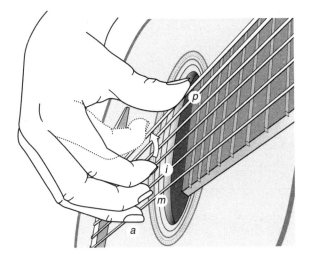

When describing the right-hand fingers, we use the initials of their Spanish names. So far we've used *p*, *i*, and *m* (*pulgar*, *indice*, and *medio*). Now we need to add *a* (*anular*), the ring finger.

When playing free-stroke pieces, use:

p   for bass notes
i   for third-string notes
m   for second-string notes
a   for first-string notes

Open-string exercises

A Plucked Chord
is a group of notes on different strings which are played together.

An Arpeggio
is a chord which is broken up, each note played in turn moving across the strings.

Free-stroke tunes using fingered notes

40: demo

Vals Triste

Trio

* **Adagio** means play slowly.

For this trio, work on Guitar 2 and 3 parts first, and then invent a slow tune for the Guitar 1 part.

Guitar 1:
Listen to parts 2 and 3, played on the CD (track 40) or by other pupils, and then start by playing one dotted minim (𝅗𝅥.) per bar and notes from the two arpeggios used in the accompaniment—E, G, and B (also try the G on string 1), or A, C, and E. Listen carefully and follow the accompaniment so that you know where the arpeggio changes. As you become more confident, try adding more notes, but keep things simple. Finally, once you've arrived at a tune you're happy with, try writing it down on the blank stave.

🔘 41: demo

Theme and Variation

Theme

Variation

Introducing F♯

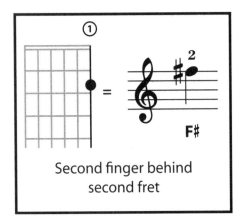

Second finger behind
second fret

The Sharp (♯)
When written before a note, this makes the note one fret
(one semitone) higher.

The sharp sign applies to all following notes on the same
line or space within the same bar, making these sharp too.

G Major Scale

Rest stroke

Try playing the scale as a two-part round. The second guitar begins when the first reaches *.

42: demo

Scale Study

Rest stroke

* Remember, this F is still sharp.

43: demo
44: accomp

(Meet) the Flintstones

Accompanied

Joseph Barbera, William Hanna,
and Hoyt Curtin

(2-bar intro)

45: demo

El Coqui
(The Tree-Frog)

Trad. (Latin-American)

Duet

The Key Signature

The previous three pieces were in the key of G, meaning they used the notes of the G major scale and that all Fs were sharpened. The usual way to indicate key is to write the relevant sharps (or flats—you'll meet these later on) at the beginning of the piece, like this:

Always look for the key signature before starting a piece of music.

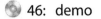 46: demo

Andante in G

Duet

Andante means play at a moderate walking pace.

A simple **ostinato** (short repeated pattern) can be added to 'Andante in G'. Try playing the descending scale C–B–A–G as one dotted minim (♩.) per bar.

🔘 47: demo

Waltz

F. Carulli

Free stroke

D.C. means go back to the beginning; **Fine** means 'the finish'.

This waltz (a popular ballroom dance in 3/4 time) can be accompanied using G and D7 chords (see Chord Diagrams, p. 60). Try to work out which chord fits which bar by listening to 🔘 track 47 and playing along.

34

Fourth-string notes

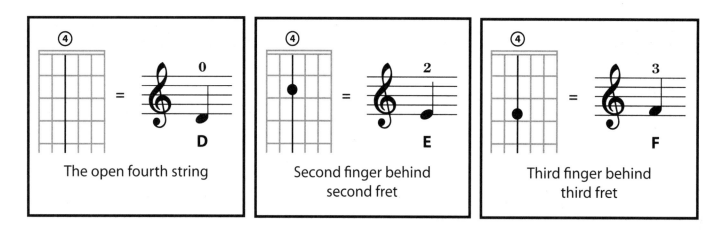

The open fourth string   Second finger behind second fret   Third finger behind third fret

Exercise

48: demo

Camelot

Duet

mf (repeat ponticello)*

* *Ponticello* means play near the bridge. It is often shortened to *pont*.

49: demo

A Blues Duet

Duet

This uses a new time signature, 6/4, meaning six crotchets (♩) to a bar. 6/4 is usually felt as two dotted minims (♩.) per bar, as you can hear in the intro clicks on the CD.

Although the fourth string is usually played with the thumb, sometimes it is better to use fingers to avoid frequent thumb/finger changes.

* Play ordinary third fret F, noting the following…

The Natural (♮)
This sign cancels out the sharp in a key signature or one occurring earlier in the bar. The natural sign applies to all following notes on the same line or space within the same bar.

50: demo

The Ash Grove

Trad.

51: demo

Shalom Chaverim

Trad. (Hebrew)

Try this piece as a round, with further guitars coming in at *. Accompany this with any of the ostinatos below. Finish on a first beat of the bar to match the tune.

1

2

3

✗ means tap the body of the guitar with the right-hand fingers.

Alternatively, accompany with a Dm chord throughout (see Chord Diagrams, p. 60), strumming strings 1 to 4.

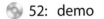 52: demo

Dreaming

pp (*pianissimo*) = very soft _____ = getting gradually softer

A gentle strummed chord can be added as a simple accompaniment, alternating each bar C, G, C, G, *etc.* Guitar 1 could try improvising on the repeat using the notes C, D, E, F, and G. Keep your rhythms similar to the written part to make your improvisation convincing.

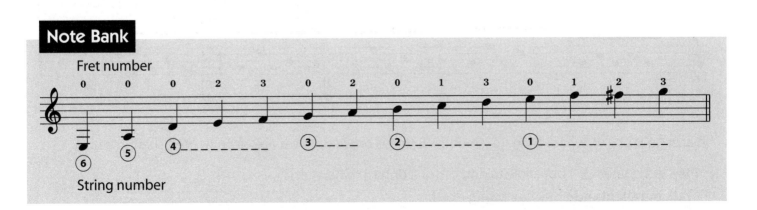

Introducing G♯

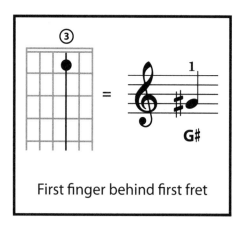

First finger behind first fret

🔘 53: demo

Invention

Rest stroke

- 'Invention' can be accompanied with just Am and E chords (see Chord Diagrams, p. 60). Work out which chord goes where by playing with another pupil or with the CD.
- 'Invention' can also be a trio, by inventing a bass-line using bass A and bass E.
- Vary the melody, e.g. by playing down rather than up the scale in bars 1 and 3 (in the repeat).

🔘 54: demo

Study in A minor

Free stroke

In arpeggio pieces, where a legato (smooth) sound is needed, voices are often written sharing a note.

* Play as a quaver (♪) but allow to ring on for a dotted minim (♩.).

** **rall.** or **rallentando** means slowing down.

55: demo

Pony Trek

Free stroke

56: demo

The Cossacks

Trio

The next piece, 'Malagueña', uses a flamenco technique where the thumb takes all the melody notes while the fingers play a repeated treble note. First, practise the open-string exercise below, using free stroke throughout:

57: demo

Malagueña

Trad. (Spanish)

Free stroke

*Strum across the strings with the thumb (*p*) from the bass to the treble.

QUIZ 2

1 Would you use a free stroke or a rest stroke for these bars of music?

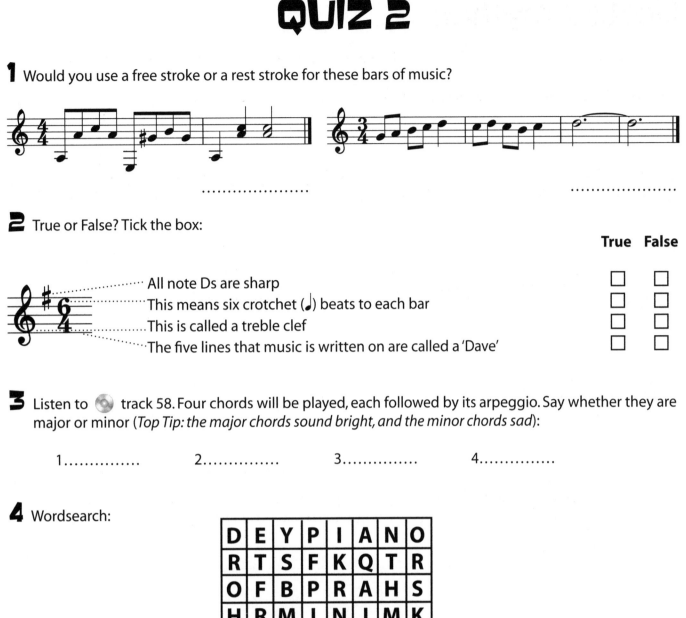

....

2 True or False? Tick the box:

True | False

All note Ds are sharp
This means six crotchet (♩) beats to each bar
This is called a treble clef
The five lines that music is written on are called a 'Dave'

3 Listen to 💿 track 58. Four chords will be played, each followed by its arpeggio. Say whether they are major or minor (*Top Tip: the major chords sound bright, and the minor chords sad*):

1............... 2............... 3............... 4...............

4 Wordsearch:

D	E	Y	P	I	A	N	O
R	T	S	F	K	Q	T	R
O	F	B	P	R	A	H	S
H	R	M	I	N	I	M	K
C	E	D	I	M	T	W	E
G	T	T	A	F	R	C	U
H	S	R	A	T	I	U	G
O	W	L	B	S	O	A	J

A note value (length) that reads the same forwards and backwards ....

What this book is all about! ....

The metal bars on the fingerboard ....

Notes played together ....

One fret higher than F is called F? ....

A repeated short phrase played over and over ....

Play softly (and a keyboard instrument) ....

A piece written for three players ....

5 Listen to 💿 track 59. The tune below will be played once as written and then again with two changes to the rhythm. Circle the two bars where the rhythm has changed:

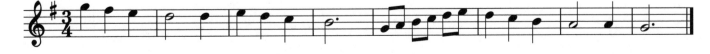

Dotted rhythms

We have already used the tie 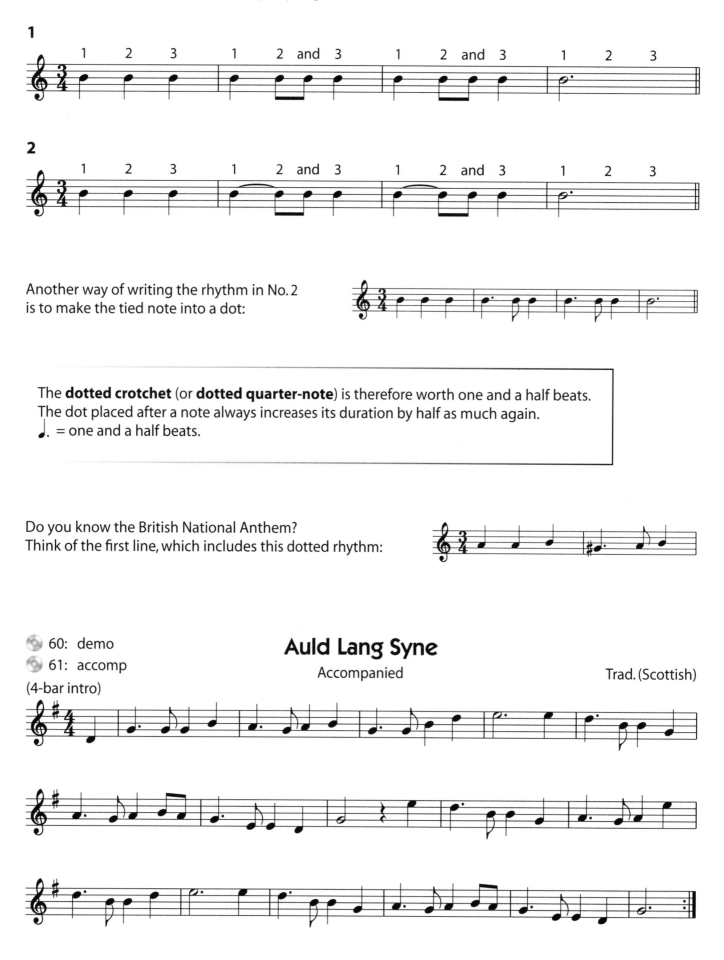, where the first note is allowed to ring for the total of the two.

Play the following exercises, counting as you go:

1

2

Another way of writing the rhythm in No. 2
is to make the tied note into a dot:

> The **dotted crotchet** (or **dotted quarter-note**) is therefore worth one and a half beats.
> The dot placed after a note always increases its duration by half as much again.
> ♩. = one and a half beats.

Do you know the British National Anthem?
Think of the first line, which includes this dotted rhythm:

60: demo
61: accomp
(4-bar intro)

Auld Lang Syne

Accompanied

Trad. (Scottish)

62: demo

The First Nowell

Trad. (French)

63: demo

The Lutenist

Duet

A third player could add percussion to 'The Lutenist' by tapping on the body of the guitar.

Try the following rhythms: ♩ ♩ ♩ or ♩ ♫ ♩

A new time signature

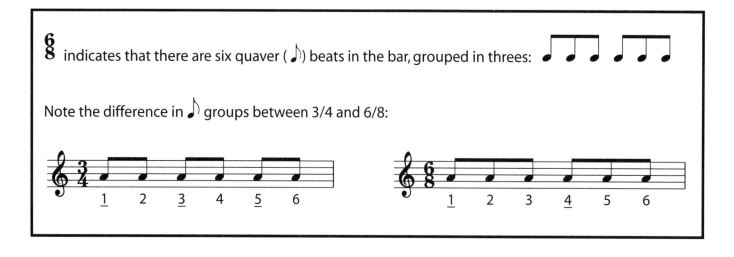

$\frac{6}{8}$ indicates that there are six quaver (♪) beats in the bar, grouped in threes:

Note the difference in ♪ groups between 3/4 and 6/8:

Try the following exercise:

6/8 is felt as two dotted crotchets (♩.) per bar, as you will hear in the intro clicks to the following pieces on the CD.

64: demo

Row, row, row your boat

Four-part round

Trad.

Once secure, try this as a round, with further guitars coming in at *. You can also accompany this with a G chord throughout.

65: demo

Irish Jig

Trad. (adapted)

66: demo

Country Jig

'Irish Jig' and 'Country Jig' can be accompanied with just G and D7 chords (see Chord Diagrams, p. 60). Work with another pupil, or with the CD, to figure out the order of the chords. Both jigs can be strung together to form a 'set': play 'Irish' (lengthening the last note to ♩), then 'Country' (shortening the last note to ♪), then back to 'Irish'.

Accidentals

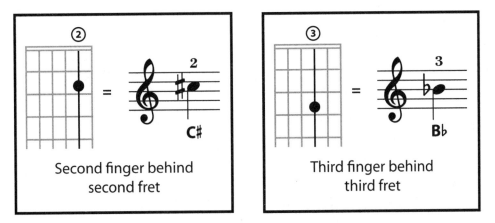

You have already used F♯ and G♯. We now need to learn C♯ and B♭, given above.

The flat sign (♭) written before a note makes it sound one fret (a semitone) lower. Sharps and flats, when introducing a change from the key signature, are known as **accidentals**.

Another accidental is the natural (♮), which we met on p. 35. As well as cancelling sharps and flats in a key signature, remember that a natural cancels sharps or flats used earlier in the bar.

67: demo

Manhattan Nights

* Allow the note to ring on.   ** Use third finger for C♯ in the final chord.

68: demo

Oasis

(**rit.** *last time*)*   **Fine**

D.C. al Fine

* **rit.** or **ritenuto** means hold back.

69: demo

Cowboy Blues

rall.

* 𝄽· = a dotted crotchet rest, worth three quavers.

Note Bank

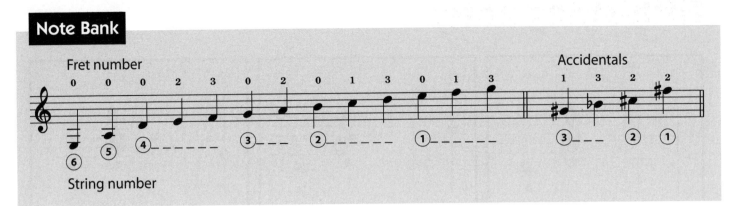

To prepare for the next piece, first practise the three-note chord progression Dm-Am-E-Am (see Chord Diagrams, p. 60).

🔘 70: demo

Turkish Dance

Fifth-string notes

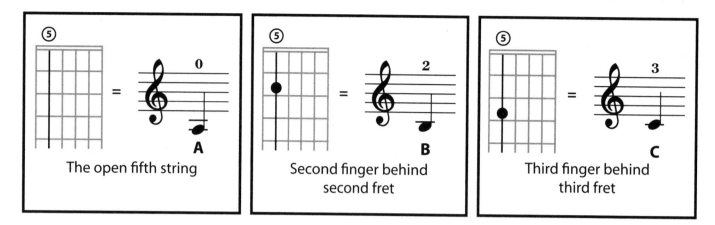

A	B	C
The open fifth string	Second finger behind second fret	Third finger behind third fret

Try the following exercise:

71: demo

Song of the Volga Boatmen

Trad. (Russian)

Adagio

Keeping with a Russian theme, work out the tune of 'The Russian Girl' (p. 20) but in a lower octave.

Begin:

Note Bank

72: demo

The Wasp

Free stroke

Allegro

Here, play the bass notes louder than the top Es, to emphasize the tune.

Allegro means fast and lively.

C Major Scale

Rest stroke

Now play as a two-part round, with the second guitar beginning when the first reaches *.

73: demo
74: accomp

Silent Night

Accompanied

Franz Grüber

(4-bar intro)

cresc. or **crescendo** means getting gradually louder.
dim. or **diminuendo** means getting gradually softer.

Playing thumb and fingers together

When playing thumb and fingers together, be careful not to let them collide. Remember to swing your thumb forwards in front of your fingers, and to take extra care to avoid pulling the strings up with *i* and *m*.

Start with the following exercise:

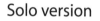

The Russian Girl

Solo version

Now try playing guitar parts 1 and 2 of the 'Barcarolle', on p. 21, simultaneously, as if it were a solo piece.

75: demo

Summer is Icumen in

Four-part round

Trad.

Once secure, play this as a round, with further guitars coming in at *. You can also accompany it with the following ostinato:

Ostinato

For an 'early music' feel, try tapping on the body of the guitar, to add percussion.

Here's an exercise using three- and four-note chords:

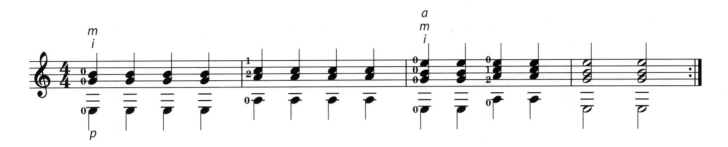

Pastoral

The second guitar part can be played with three- or four-note chords. If you prefer to play three-note chords, just leave out the top E.

🔘 76: demo

Duet

Sixth-string notes

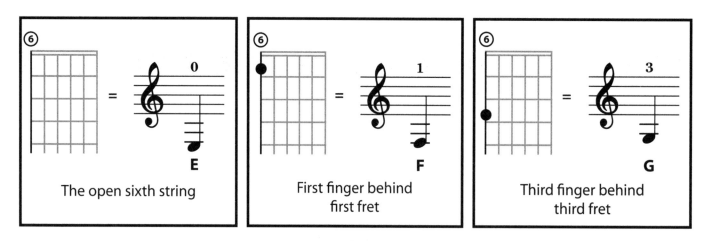

The open sixth string

First finger behind first fret

Third finger behind third fret

Start with the following exercise:

77: demo

Siesta

More work on bass notes

Try working out a simple bass-line to 'Happy Birthday' (which we played on p. 24), using bass C, G, and F. You can use one dotted minim (𝅗𝅥.) per bar or a mixture of crotchet (♩), minim (𝅗𝅥), and dotted minim (𝅗𝅥.) beats.

Now work out 'London's Burning' (p. 24) in the lower octave, beginning:

E minor Pentatonic Scale

🔘 78: demo

The Condor

Here, improvise using the notes of the E minor pentatonic scale. Practise the scale first, then play the piece, making up your own melody in the blank bars (5–8 and 13–16).

Accompany 'The Condor' with a full, strummed Em chord, using a pattern such as:

Strum with the index finger from the treble to the bass, and then tap the body of the guitar with the thumb above the strings.

More playing in two parts/voices

🔘 79: demo

Three in One

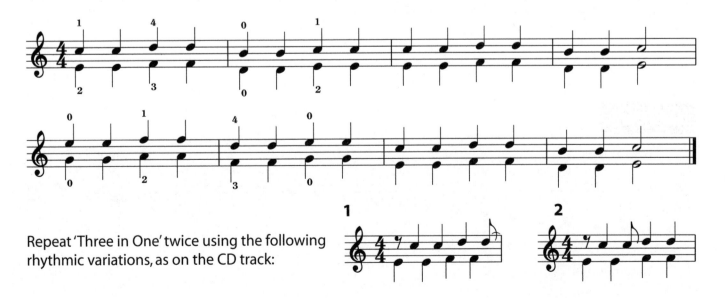

Repeat 'Three in One' twice using the following rhythmic variations, as on the CD track:

🔘 80: demo
🔘 81: accomp

(2-bar intro)

Two's Company
Accompanied

🔘 82: demo

The Coventry Carol

Trad.

Note Bank

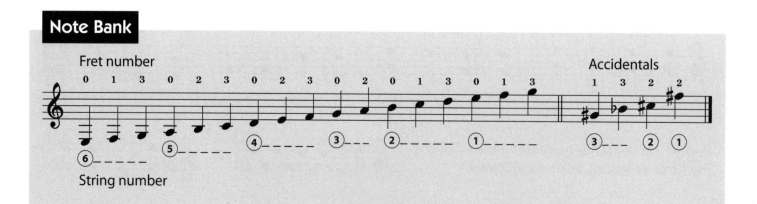

🔘 83: demo

Andante in C

Giuliani
arr. D. Cracknell

Duet

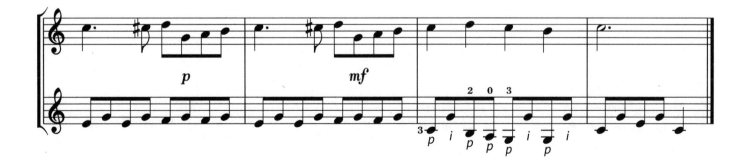

Another F♯ and C♯

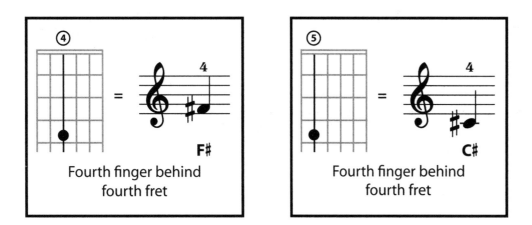

Play the following exercises:

1

2

84: demo

Greensleeves

Trad.

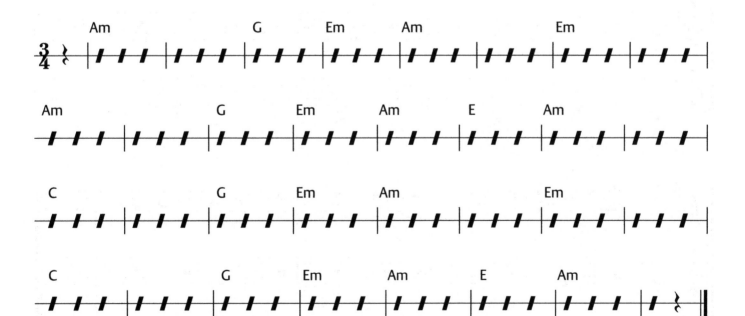

This can be played as a solo (as written), as a duet (tune and chords, or tune and bass-line), or as a trio (tune, bass, and chords). Play the chords with a gentle strum or as an arpeggio (see Chord Diagrams, p. 60).

85: demo

Match of the Day

Barry Stoller

Trio

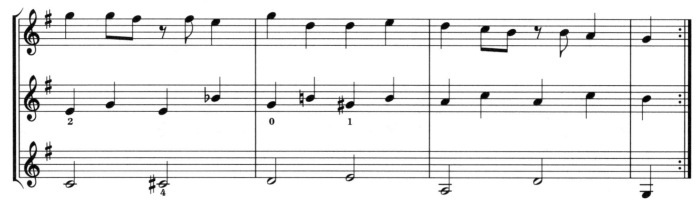

QUIZ 3

1 Fill in the letter names for the three fingers and thumb on the right hand:

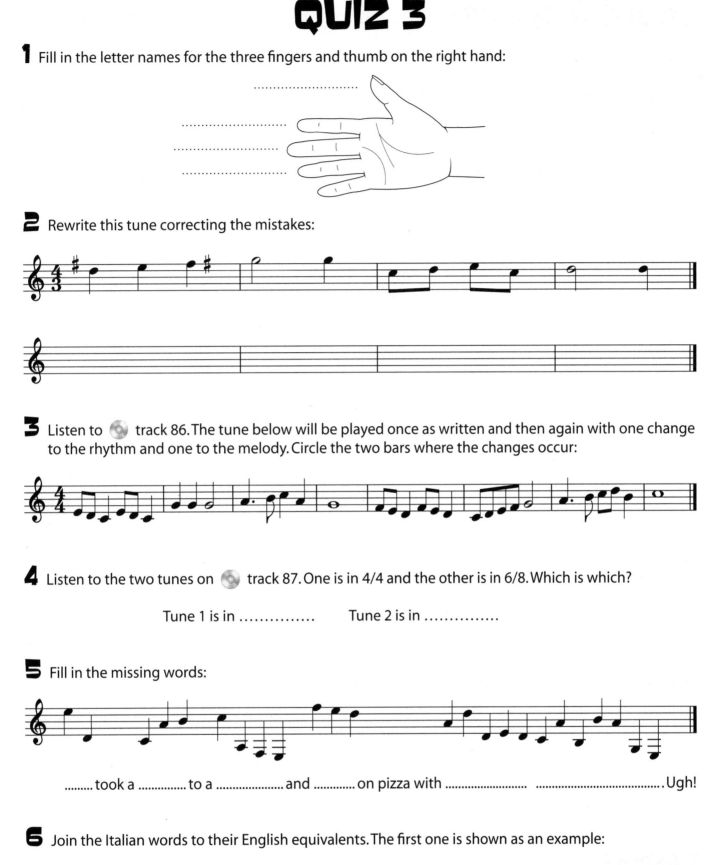

2 Rewrite this tune correcting the mistakes:

3 Listen to ⊙ track 86. The tune below will be played once as written and then again with one change to the rhythm and one to the melody. Circle the two bars where the changes occur:

4 Listen to the two tunes on ⊙ track 87. One is in 4/4 and the other is in 6/8. Which is which?

Tune 1 is in ……………   Tune 2 is in ……………

5 Fill in the missing words:

……… took a …………… to a ………………… and ………… on pizza with ……………………… ……………………………………. Ugh!

6 Join the Italian words to their English equivalents. The first one is shown as an example:

ponticello	play loudly
andante	broken chord
allegro	the finish
a maestro	play near the bridge
rallentando	play slowly
forte	play quickly
adagio	walking pace
arpeggio	what you'll be with practice!
Fine	slowing down

Chord Diagrams

There are three types of chord on this page:

- a letter on its own means the chord is **major**, a bright-sounding chord using notes 1, 3, and 5 of the major scale;
- a letter plus 'm' means the chord is **minor**, a sad-sounding chord using notes 1, 3, and 5 of the minor scale;
- and a letter plus '7' indicates a major chord with an added note, the 7th degree of the scale.

Three-note chords (try not to hit strings ④ ⑤ ⑥):

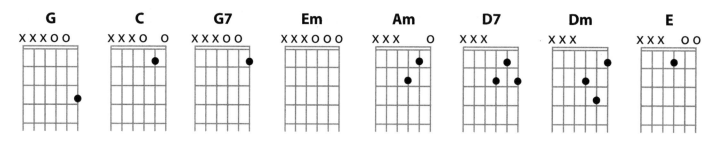

Full versions of the chords:

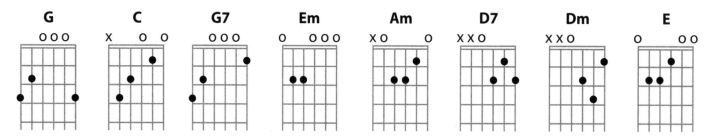

Eight chord windows for your/your teacher's chords:

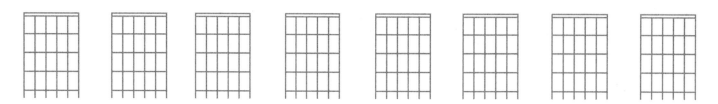

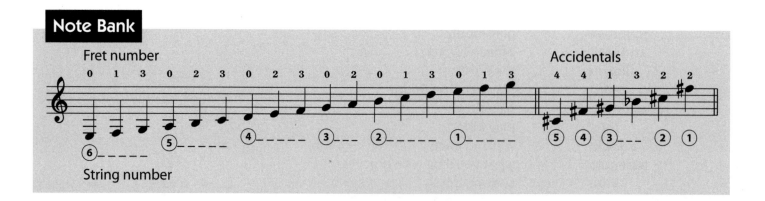

Manuscript

Practice Register

Date

Date

Date
